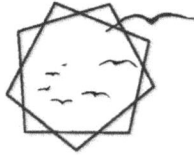

I Begin

I Begin

POETRY AND PRAYERS

OF A WOMAN'S JOURNEY

THROUGH GRIEF AND LOSS

GINNY GASKILL

ISBN: 978-1-940769-30-1
Publisher: Mercury HeartLink
Printed in the United States of America

Contact the author at:
ggaskill46@comcast.net
ginnyschaos.blogspot.com

Mercury HeartLink
www.heartlink.com

Contents

FIRST SECTION

— CHAPTER ONE —

— Chapter Two —

— Chapter Three —

— CHAPTER FOUR —

SECOND SECTION

ACKNOWLEDGMENTS

I want to thank Richard Hiester. Who walked with me when I could barely put one foot in front of the other. He was my rock in a sea of grief. He would say "You lead, I follow." And he did. But he threw brilliant pebbles in front of me so I would stop, scoop them up, and keep going.

He introduced me to C. G. Jung, <u>The Red Book,</u> Bill Plotkin, <u>Soulcraft,</u> Chaim Potok, <u>My Name Is Asher Lev,</u> Dan Millman, <u>The Way Of The Peaceful Warrior,</u> and many others.

The most powerful for me was <u>Soulcraft</u> by Bill Plotkin. He led me to where I could cradle my soul in my own arms. His book was full of poetry, David Whyte, Rumi, Rilke, and Mary Oliver. I went out and bought books by these poets and I was transformed.

One day I wrote. I did not know where it came from. A month later the words came flowing from me. Now they do not stop and I am grateful for voice.

I am full of appreciation for Janice Rautman. She edited my words, helping me find clarity and the right words when I went askew. She translated both the French and Spanish versions of my poetry that appear in this volume. This book would not have been the same without her input.

Stewart Warren, my publicist, did not give up on me. I thought I was ready for this when I was not. He talked me down off of my ledge of grief. At times my words were clumsy and he gave me time to correct, get my bearings and balance again. Thank you, Stewart.

I thank my new Albuquerque poetry friends who encouraged me to write and read at public gatherings and believed my stringing of words had value. This is an unbelievable community. There are so many of you and so many unique voices out there.

PREFACE

A while ago, feels like once upon a time, my life was pretty ordinary. I was married, had children, stepchildren, and a multitude of grandchildren. My faith was strong. I loved and worked in many types of art. My home was more than adequate, and I loved my garden. My husband Bill, was ill, so I was a caregiver, but he was kind and generous, and loved me to distraction, so I considered myself blessed.

During this time, I worked with a psychotherapist, Richard Hiester, who helped me through the care-taking and other trials and tribulations in my life. I worked through past abuses and wounds, the ones we all experience, but which are so unique to each one of us.

In December 2012, my world began to unravel. My granddaughter, Marta, at age 17, took her life. I thought my heart would break. She was so smart, beautiful, inside and out. She had so much potential, so much to live for. Why? And there was no answer. We guessed, we blamed, we cried. One day here then, the next: all the potential, the dreams, exploded, gone. All we were left with was our grief. I held my family, the best I knew how. I cried and I cried, and cried and then cried more. The tears formed a pool, that flowed out of me. It was more of a shimmer, like the mirages one sees in the desert.

Bill began to get sick. On New Year's Eve I took him to the hospital and three weeks later he died. My beliefs are strong and so were his. I knew he would be safe in God's arms. Bill had been sick so long that, even though I knew I would miss him, I believed I would feel relief that he was no longer in pain. He had suffered for most of twenty years. I was wrong. I held him in my arms as he took his last breath, and told him to go find Marta, and her dog Abby. That I would come later. That it was all right.

To this day when I think of them, they are in a wildflower meadow, sitting in the grasses. There is a pine tree to the left of Marta, and Bill is on her right. Abby, a Great Pyrenees, Marta's dog, lies at their feet. Abby died a month before Marta did. This is my image and it sustains me.

During this time my faith held me. I would be lying to say I was not angry at my loss. I was. But I had been blessed in my teenage years to have had an encounter with the Holy Spirit and no matter how angry I get, I cannot deny. It was a gift in a time of need and it still sustains me after fifty years.

One day, when my grief was so great, I was sitting in Richard's office. My heart was broken, my soul cried out, and I felt like I could bear no more. Why did I hurt so much? How could I hurt so much? I could have fallen into a hole and pulled the earth in over me, and I would have felt, been justified.

He told me a story. He held up his hands, thumbs up, about nine inches apart. He said, "Ginny, most people live between this space. They spend their whole life here. It is where they are safe. So this is how much they can hurt, but it is also how much they can love, and live. They wonder why things do not get better, it is because they have not allowed the room." He told me that this grief was so much better for me, that it would knock out one side and the other would have to move as well. To be open, to give it time. That this is a constant balancing act. I only get one if I accept the other.

I trusted Richard, I listened. I let the grief, the pain, the fear wash over and through me. That was my first lesson in opening. I still learn from that one. How to allow myself to feel in the pain, to let it happen. To allow the tears that would not stop, the sobs that tore through my chest. My mind, played with the images of the past, letting them come. Each time these feelings flowed over me, my walls widened. My walls are canyon walls of sandstone, maybe because they can be worn down. They are the beautiful reds and creams of the Southwest. Today they are wide apart. Wild poppies, golden, cover the floor of the valley. I wander my path to and fro. It is of contentment, though the tears still fall. There is truth now, my own truth. I will do my best to live it, one day, one step, at a time.

One day, if we are lucky, our world will be rocked, and if we open ourselves, our lives will never be the same. A marriage to your beloved, the birth of a child can do this, and that is opening with love: wonder at what you have been blessed with, and have created. But I believe more of it comes from sorrow, from grief. The death of that beloved. The child that should be with you, now gone. It is the lying in the ashes of your world as it burns to the ground. It is grief and total despair as never before. It is the tears and tearing of your soul.

I thought my heart, my soul, would break, that I could not bear to live the pain. I learned different ways. I now feel with a different part of me. Now, I believe, it is with soul. The year of the deaths of those I loved, I wanted to die, but I also wanted to live. The opposites written about in The Prophet, joy and sorrow.

What I did not expect was that the memories of the care-giving would slip to non-importance. The memories are of him, before the sickness took over. His strength, standing tall, his smile, the sound of his laughter, his gentleness.

In January I had passed the one year mark of Marta's death and I was approaching Bill's. I was nervous, did not feel right. Richard had said I needed a year. To not let others fill my life. To just be, to take it a little at a time. I was lonely and insanely tired. I felt I had died inside.

I began to feel something, a moment, and then it was gone. I kept reaching for it and it would find me. It was a flicker, but it wanted to be heard. It tried to find its way, insisted on its way. This thing, this moment, would not leave me alone. It struck me under my ribs and said, "I am here. Pay attention to me, feel me", and then it was gone. I thought and I talked and I said, "This feeling is like a "quickening" in my soul". Did I say that out loud, or was it a thought? I don't know, it doesn't matter, but I found my word, quickening. It is the spark, the beginning of life, the feeling of rebirth.

There was movement in that quickening place. Part of me said, get up and get busy. The other said, stay still and write. Find out what you are feeling, both in body and soul. If you do this, you will be stronger, more authentic. So there I stayed, for a little while. Was this quickening the beginning of finding the soul? It wanted to feel. I felt it in my breast. It wanted to burst out and in that quickening place said "me first". One pulled inside me and the other screamed to be free. I needed to pay attention to the quickening. A mustard seed under my ribs.

The day I felt that quickening, was the real beginning. Hunting, searching, fighting my way. It probably was a good thing I did not understand much and just trusted. If I had known how hard it would be, I might have said "No." What I would have lost.

That winter, each morning, I built a fire, sat in front of it on a leather sofa, pulled steamer trunks up on each side. I created my own cocoon. For two months I studied C. G. Jung's, <u>The Red Book</u>, and Bill Plotkin's, <u>Soulcraft</u>. The stuff was so over my head but I found the will to go forward to try to understand "soul encounter." I was fascinated by Plotkin's work. I did not believe I had the skill to do what he asked of me, but I could not put it down. I have read this book seven times already. I wrote ferociously. Filling volume after volume, trying to put words down, to capture what I was feeling.

One night I dreamed of flowers and sexuality. It was a soft pretty dream that I did not understand. It kept repeating itself and I finally told Richard. We began to analyze it. Each piece, each flower had a meaning and that is a story in itself. Because of this dream I went through fire and ice. I held my soul in my hands, cradled it to my body. I watched my spirit soar. My first soul encounter, frightening and beautiful in the same moment.

In May, I traveled to Oregon to be by myself. I knew I needed to grow. My soul cried for release. I spent a month in a little old motel. Here the forest met the sea, and I felt at home. I walked the beach, followed creeks, touched the foam of the sea with my toes. Trees and flowers bloomed and gave forth their scent. Animals came, watched me with doe-eyed quiet and angular haunches.

The first day in Oregon I started to write and it came out as poetry. Where this came from I don't know, but I embraced it and I have not stopped. I loved the rhythm of the words, their cadence. I laughed and cried, and marveled at the words as they appeared on paper. During that month I had four more soul encounters. They were of soul, sexuality and abuse. Again another story for another time.

This volume of poetry contains the first eight months of my conscious writing. I found a few poems written earlier in my journals and I have added them to this mix. But mostly, it is my writing from spring into winter of that year. I hope you enjoy my story. The beginning of my voice. It is time for me to shush. I have said enough and as poets say, it is time to. . .

    Speak Poet Speak

In Memory of Bill Gaskill, my husband

Thank you,
for bringing
love's light
to my eyes.

To Richard Hiester, my friend

Thank you,
for picking
it up
and handing
it back
to me

FIRST SECTION

I should advise you to put it all down as beautifully as you can – in some beautifully bound book. It will seem as if you were making the vision banal – but then you need to do that – then you are freed from the power of them. If you do that with these eyes for instance they will cease to draw you. You should never try to make the visions come again. Think of it in your imagination and try to paint it. Then when these things are in some precious book you can go back to the book and turn over the pages and for you it will be your church – your cathedral – the silent places of your spirit where you will find renewal. If anyone tells you that it is morbid or neurotic and you listen to them – then you will lose your soul – for in that book is your soul.

Christina Morgan recalling Jung's words
Carl G. Jung The Red Book

— Chapter One —

The minute I heard my first love story
I started looking for you, not knowing
how blind that was.
Lovers don't finally meet somewhere.
They're in each other all along.

Jelaluddin Rumi <u>The Essential Rumi</u>
—from "Music Master"

SOFTNESS AND STRENGTH

The softness of a woman
gives a man
a soft place
to land upon.

The strength of a man
holds her,
keeps her from
falling.

Your Last Breath

For six days I held you.
Held your hand in daylight.
Lay beside you at night
my arm across you.

Not wanting you to be alone.
Not knowing hour to hour
if that breath
would be your last.

How would I breathe
after your last one?
I did not want to know
I just needed to hear you breathe.

I Do Not Begrudge, I Miss

I do not begrudge him
his time of rest.
He earned it.

But I miss the boyish man.
I want the goofy grin,
and the stance
of that man.

I miss the smallness
of my hand
in his.

CARE-GIVING SUCKS

the fucking gone.
Moments of emotional
intimacy still remain.

We are bound to that love
built on a promise
given in our prime.

Unforgettable
mountain meadow love.
It holds us
in arms of grass, of yarrow.
The wind ruffling our passion.
Never letting us forget.
Reminding us with
each new breath.

I clean the crumbs,
the blood from the wall.
Try to erase
where he took that fall.

Once I waited
for his touch each night.

Now I listen.
Pray, he will not fall
will get to the bathroom
in time.

Hold my breath
till he lies down, again.

He sleeps.
I cannot.
I am so tired.

HOSPICE

Every week I took –
   apples
      oranges
         grapes
            or berries
to hospice.

To this place where Bill died.
I had needed food that was
not heavy while I watched him.
Could not stand the cloying sweet
of cookies and pastries.
Needed food of life.

So now I take –
   apples
      oranges
         grapes
            or berries
to hospice.

My journey completed,
so many must follow.
I know they need that
sweet clear honey
on their tongues.
They still have to live
while they endure their journey.

So I will bring –
   apples
      oranges
         grapes
            or berries
to hospice.

WHAT CAN I SAY

I do not mourn his passing.
So many times
he should have gone.
But he stayed
because he would not,
could not, leave me.
What can I say?
He believed
I was his sun.

It's Tuesday Morning

It's Tuesday morning.
I seek release.
My body cries.
My soul tormented.
I sob out loud.
I cannot bare
this aloneness.

I Want Him Beside Me

Richard says it seems
like I am doing well.
And I agree.

I have friends, family.
I travel, write poetry
see tiny bits of life
through my words.

But what do I do
with the longing?
The one that has no name.

After all this time,
I still do not understand.

How can I miss
something so fleeting
so long ago?

I miss to my core.
My soul cries out.
My heart aches.

I want him beside me –
    fighting wars
      gardening
        in my bed.

Maybe, I am all right.
My essence is strong.
My voice can be heard.

I am content
except when I am not.

He Reaches for My Hand

He reaches for my hand
sometimes landing on my knee.

He holds us
together as we walk,
sitting on the side of our bed.
He brings it to his lips
in a gentle kiss.

Always ending with his hand
wrapped around mine.
I feel small, but not diminished.

I am cocooned. I am safe.
He protects my imaginal buds.
He gives me wings.

My Laments 1

My Lord,
From my loins
come the flames.
I am afraid.
I want to love
to feel
to create.
I need to live
before I die.

I cry to my God.
Oh God,
I love you.
I know not to whom I speak.
I cannot define Him.
I only know
of my universal
love for Him.

Oh my soul,
I am afraid of your power.
If I touch you
will you die?
If I don't, will I?

SHARDS OF RAIN

I hear Richard's
sweet voice
"Find the joy in the sadness."

But today
I cannot.
My heart is heavy.

Shards, slivers
of pain fall
like rain.
Cut me with each drop.

His Fingertips

His fingers so wide
I cannot slip mine
between.

So I hang onto the tips.
Smile, happy inside.

He curls around
enfolds my hand.
I am cocooned
safe for the day.

When I have grieved enough,
he will open that hand
and let me soar.

I'VE NEVER SEEN A FLOWER LIKE THAT

We drove down the highway
in that blue truck.
He called her Betsy.
Windows down
hair blowing
from desert scented air.

I was content, lazy.
Sun on my face.
Could a day be
any better?
I watched the cactus
the sage slip by.
I say,
"I've never seen a flower like that."

Brakes squeal.
Seat-belt holds me from the dash.
Tires slide on pebbles.

Memories flood
I am afraid.
I remember in my remembering
being hit, berated
for my thoughts,
beaten for not
anticipating his.

I head for my rabbit hole.
I need to hide.
I cry out
"What's wrong?"

This man, this lover
calmly says,
"You wanted to see that flower."
and he backs up the truck.

I melted.
I knew.
I could love this man,
love him forever
and I did.

When the loneliness
becomes too great and
I feel I will die
I see the smile in his eyes
and his voice
"You wanted to see that flower."

Drowned by Tears

My heart broke
as love was snatched away
pulled out of my grip.

I was bereft
my heart broke.
I lay in my grief
drowned by tears.

He Is Breath

He is breath upon my skin.
I feel his kiss upon me.
He lingers as he slides
across my life.

I loved this man.
Still love him.
The essence of him
will caress my body
invade my soul,
forever.

I Want to Tell Him

I want to tell him
there was more good than hard.
That I will always remember
that last I love you,
and the last soft kiss.

I want him to know I saw
that single snowflake.
The one, only for my eyes.
His gift to me.

Then the snow! Oh glorious snow!
On that sunny May afternoon.
We ran out, we laughed.
Our children, our grandchildren danced.
They knew.
He had just gifted them.

The patch of blue, and his smile.
I heard his soft voice.
The words "Go and live"
are letting me.
He says "I am okay."
And now I am too.
It gives me peace.
I just want him to know.

DESEO CONTARLE

Deseo contarle
había más de lo bueno que lo difícil.
Que siempre recordaré
ésa última te amo,
y el último beso suave.

Deseo que él sepa que ví
ese único capo de nieve.
El uno, sólo para mis ojos.
Su regalo a mí.

¡Entonces la nieve! ¡Ay, la nieve gloriosa!
En esa tarde solarosa en mayo.
Corrimos afuera, nos reímos.
Nuestras hijas, nuestros nietos bailaron.
Ellos sabían.
Él acaba de regalarles a ellos.

El área de azul, y su sonrisa.
Oí su voz suave.
Las palabras — vaya y vive—
Están dejándome.
Él dice —estoy bien.—
Y ahora yo estoy bien también.
Me da la paz.
Sólo le quiero saberlo.

MARTA

She took her life,
left a hole in ours
we cannot fill.

I grieve for her
for her mother
her brother
and for me.

I cried, still cry
for them both
and for my loss.

For the knowing—
I will never
hold her again.

That the children
she would have had
will never be.

Maybe
it was Lisa's grief,
so much worse
than mine.

Or Carl watching
his mother change
before his very eyes.

I could not desert them.
I held them
the best I knew how.

I cried and cried
and cried some more
and then I cried again.

The tears form a pool
that flows from my heart.
This emptiness touches everything I see.
A mirage upon my desert.

I cannot ask, how it can heal.
It is a wound that cuts inside.

Time will blunt the knife.
It will scab over, calcify
harden that part.

And I will live and grow.
Be open to this.
My life will fill again.
But always,
hold onto that part.

Is It Too Much to Ask

I am angry, hurt inside.
Is it too much to ask?
I just want that moment

to relive
the scent of pine and earth.
I want to taste
my lover's mouth.
Drink deep.

Taste his honeyed lips
and the salt of his skin.
Is it too much to ask?

Please Let Me Sleep

I lie here.
Pretend to sleep
pad of paper, pen
lay next to me.

I've turned on
the light.
The darkness
does not
let me rest.

Thoughts come
unbidden to
my head, my hand.

I want to sleep.
Please
let me sleep.

THREE YOUNG MEN
to Collin, Weston, Mathew

Three young men
moved in next door.
College kids—
they were smart, athletic
good-looking, and kind.
But the neighbors said
party too hardy,
too many friends.

But I,
I know them differently.
The shovel taken from my hands.
The sweetness, the caring
of an old woman and her man.

Bill, so frail.
They stopped to speak
and listen. They gave
him honor, dignity.

He watched these men
as they came to play
they swam, they laughed.
We loved their ways.

One day Bill spoke
"I wish, I could go in."

They asked. "Why not?"
He sighed
"Can get in, can't get out."

They said with a grin
"Come on, really?"
They flexed their muscles.
Grinned again.

I watched his excitement
      the slow move
            from wheelchair
                  to walker
                        walker to stairs.
Then to that cooling water.

I saw the joy on his face.
I almost cried.
They stayed so close.
They took such care.

I will never forget
till the day I die.
Three young men
who brought light
to his eyes.

Our Chalice

We gave from our hearts.
Gathered with our souls.
Our chalice was filled
to overflowing.

Full enough to sustain us
in our time of despair.
And still
there was enough left
to prime me.

To begin
to fill my well again.
To not leave me
empty and dry.

My Granddaughter
in Memory of Marta

How do I tell
the story of a
child with gray blue eyes
and hair of burnished copper?
She, only here a little while.

So many memories,
feelings I cannot contain.
They spill –
   from my eyes
      my heart
         my fingers.

How do you capture
a child whose pink
is light red or magenta?

She walked her own talk –
   Strong
      opinionated
         compassionate
           caring.

Loved everything with fur and wings.
She picked up bugs, reptiles
marveled at the differences
and reasons for being.

She loved her mother.
Learned to love
a brother for his own right.

I remember –

"Look Grandma, contrail."
A tiny little girl
pointing to the sky.

Walking on the beach.
Her absorbing everything –
   each shell
      each animal
she encounters.

Mimicking animal sounds
not meow or bow wow.
Each sound unique to her.
Made me laugh with delight.

I would give anything
to hear her voice.
"Grandma can I come swim?"
"Can I bring friends too?"

I wish I could
hold her hand
in mine again.
The tiny one that could
only hold one finger.
The one that grasped

mine so she would
not fall.

This little girl sat sewing.
Hands holding bits of cotton
as she fed them
into the mouth
of a sewing machine.

The long slender fingers
of a teenage artist.
Watching her create,
sharing paint and brushes,
brought joy to my life.

Remembering her gentleness
with her Papa.
Her tender touch.
He loved her so much.

Be with God my child.
I love you.
Save a place
for your mother and me
close by you.
Go in peace.

Your Grandma

Beneath My Skin

My emotions are just
beneath my skin.

My body barely able
to contain them.

What happens
if they escape,
take wing?

COMING DOWN

The body not able
to contain.
Fire flying
from fingertips
   touching
      petting skin
         pushing hair
no longer pulling.

The screams hushed
   racked breathing
      gulps for air
         chest heaving
            skin quivering.
Eyes open
seeing breath
smiling.
Fingers touch lips
lips suck fingers.
Words
   forbidden
      curling into
     around
         contentment
        sleep.

CLOSE YOUR EYES, BREATHE DEEP

Close your eyes.
Yes, I really mean
close your eyes.

Breathe soft, slow
again
and again.
Breathe deep, long
let it go.

Now, dream with me.
The air cool, crisp.
The sun warm, not hot.

Listen, hear
the sound of water
tumbling over stones
swishing around logs
as it makes its journey
to the sea.
Always forward
no sound of retreat.

Hear the wind in the pine.
Feel it on your skin.
Listen to the sparrows,
the finches,
their tiny cries of joy.

Hear the raucous sound of crow.
Keep your eyes closed
but look
he sits on the crag above you.
Inky black, he mocks you
makes you laugh.

Look down
see the golden path.
See your bare feet.
Do you see the other pair?
Are they larger
or smaller than yours?
Do you feel the grass
between your toes?

Look around
see the meadow,
white, yellow, green, hints of purple.

Lover's hand in yours.
Lie down.
Smell the yarrow
and the daisies.
Mix their musky scent with
the sweet scent of broken grass.

The grass that cushions,
beds your bodies.
Smell your lover's scent.
Chew a blade of grass.
Lie back, feel the sun.

Undo buttons
let sun invade those parts
not seen by others.

Tickle with that blade
till they grab your hand
make you stop.
Pin your hands
to your side.
Kisses that start sweet
turn deep
and you drink them in.

Hands, mouth, body
mix, move.
Create their own melody
of feels, tastes and sounds.

Sweet sound of violin
of flute.
Hands stroke strings of guitar.
The drum rolls
the beat hardens.
The crescendo.
The swish of the snare
and then, blessed sleep.

Sleep in the bed of grass
covered by the breeze
warmed by the sun
serenaded by the sounds
of nature's breath.

Sleep my lovers
sleep.

— CHAPTER TWO —

Flare up flames
and make big shadows I can move in.

Let everything happen to you: beauty and terror.
Just keep going. No feeling is final.
Don't let yourself loose me.

Rainer Maria Rilke <u>Rilke's Book of Hours,</u>
<u>Love Poems to God</u>

STRENGTH OF THE ROSE

Our love is petals of roses
folded inside.

Each time
we come together
we grow.
Unfurl into a full blown rose.
Watch out for the thorns.

As time marches on
the petals must fall.
The beauty will fade
but the strength of the rose
is in his hips and roots.

So shall be our love
always, forever.

THE SOUND OF THE CART

I want to laugh, to cry.
But outward
out of the past.

The cry is not born of tears.
It is the sound of the cart
moving from the deep rut
it has been lying in
for years.

I feel the wrenching
of the muscles,
as they work –
    to pull
        to push
            forward.

LIFE'S TIME

A little boy dances.
He laughs
holds out his hand
to the giggle.

She touches him
draws in his laugh
and giggles.

He reaches to
this child in white
and dances.
She knows him,
laughs, dances with
and around him.

Always touching
never holding
always laughing
through the giggle.

&

He stands there of
his earthen white.
He is her strength.
he sways and dances
he smiles.

She touches his hand
and dances
always around him.
He spins her
faster and faster.
They grow
with every turn.

Her gown is colored
by the sand
the canyon walls.
She is the whirl.
She laughs for joy.

ဆ

The time has passed
he stands and guards.
His arms are out
to catch her.

She lies
back to him
he does not hold her.
His touch is
but a breeze.
He is
just there.

She is so frail
still she dances.
She sways, she turns

so slowly
always with the beat.

Her gown is rendered
to ribbons of light.
They move
in his breeze.
She dances
she smiles.

A Piece of Laughter

Have you ever been so broken
that you could not look up?
Stooped to pick up
a piece of laughter.
Put it on,
and laughed
till your face hurt?

LITTLE THOUGHTS

What are these little thoughts?
They will not stop.
They buzz in my mind.
They keep me from sleep.
I am so tired
and still they stir.

They want voice.
They say listen
I have so much to tell.
You forgot to listen.
Now, you must tell my tales.

How? They do not care.
Only that I do.
That their voice is finally heard,
so they may stop
and find time to sleep.

A Single Flower

A single flower
be it rose or daisy
creates the spark.
Lights the candle
buried in my heart.

My heart beats
pushes life's blood
through my limbs
which want to hold you,
pull you to my breast.
Feel your heart
beat in time with mine.

Love ignites
from a single flower.

So Much to Learn

How do those who write –
  so eloquently
    so lyrically
      with such breadth
do it?

My writing is like –
  wisps of wind
    bursts of rain
      a sunspot
        not the whole sun.
          It is the soft
          of that first snow.

I am an infant in this writing game.
So much to learn.
So much to learn.

I Touch the Tree

It is still, here in the pines.
There is a hush.
I came to talk.
To speak to him.

To tell him. I miss him.
The children are fine.
I tell him of all the things
that were our lives.

I touch the tree.
Feel its bark, hard, rough.
It gives me grit.

I begin to tell of finding
my soul
traversing creeks.
I tell of pieces of light
I have left in trees.
Of children that need,
of frogs that croak.
The things he might
have done with me.

It is time.
I must move on.
To blend those thoughts.
To hold the past
embrace the now
to hope for my tomorrow.

Toco el Árbol

Es tranquilo, aquí en los pinos.
Hay silencio.
Vine para hablar.
Hablar a él.

Contarle. Le echo de menos.
Las hijas están bien.
Le cuento de todas las cosas
que eran nuestra vida.

Toco el árbol.
Siento su corteza, dura, aspera.
Me da valor.

Empiezo a contar de encontrar
mi alma
atravesando ríachuelos.
Cuento de pedazos de luz
que he dejado en árboles.
De niños que necesitan,
ranas que croan.
Las cosas que él posiblemente
hubiera sido conmigo.

Es la hora.
Tengo que avanzar.
Mezclar los pensamientos.
Agarrar el pasado
abrazar el ahora
Esperar mi mañana.

I Want

I want to write on the beach,
in all the wild of the Oregon coast.

I want to smell the salt air.
Have my nose wrinkle
at the putrid smell of seaweed
crabs and shells.

I want to feel the sting of sand
as it whips from the beach.

I want to touch the foam
and hear the cries of the gulls.

I want the rhythmic pull
of the waves, and the boom
of them, crashing upon the shore.

I want the sun, it entices me.
My mind can feel the warmth
on my body, my limbs.
Even my palms, my fingers
want this.

I want. I want to feel
the cool warmth of the sand
and the sea, on my feet.

All That I Need

Oh God
I ask for light
you show me the dark.
I beg for understanding
you give me questions.
I hunger
you tell me to fast.
I long for peace
you hand me the wild.
Thank you God
for giving me all that I need.

THE WISH

I wish to sleep.
I wish to dream.
Be careful
of what you wish.
You may receive.

The dreams will call you
demand of you
hold you in their grip.
Tantalizing
terrifying
they toy with you.

Forcing you to look
to your soul.
What is there?
Everything.

TREMBLING

I lie here
trembling.
I have written
my today stories.
Still, I tremble
I am not done.

I understand
the trembling –
   of love
      of sex
         anxiety
            of adrenaline.

But why this
trembling?
This thing
in the core
of me?

THE RING FINGER

He placed the band of gold
and diamonds upon my hand
twenty-five years ago.
He promised to love me forever
but he did not realize his forever
was not so long as mine.

I wore that ring with pride and honor.
The time came to put it aside.
To begin to live outside that vow.

I sat beside the fire last winter
and worked to take it off.
With tears and lotion I worked it
until it became free of the hand.
Free of the promise of forever.

The mark was ugly, deformed,
naked in its truth, and I cried.
Now, almost a year later
I look at that finger and wonder
if the mark will ever fade.

It is like the slash on the aspen.
The scars of that tree are part
of its beauty, but they never go away.

My hand is deformed, changed
by that band of gold,
the indentation still there.

I feel like I have gone
into a bar to cheat.
Taken the ring off so no one knows
of my commitment.
But everyone does know
by the mark on my hand.
That deformed ring finger.

My Laments 2

Oh God,
I am afraid of its beauty.
If I touch it
will it die?
If I don't will I?

God,
Give me strength.
I do not know
where I am going.
How will I know
when I arrive?
Oh, I know.
I will die.

I Like the Words

I begin to speak
in metaphors.
My mind flashes pictures,
thinks in prose.

It slows me down
but clarifies.

I like the words
roll them with my tongue.

I hear myself speak.
Find smoothness
in the cadence.

It whispers through the mist.
Finds its truth, its voice.
Through the black clouds
of storms, or
the heat of the sun.

— CHAPTER THREE —

Sometimes everything
 has to be
  inscribed across
   the heavens

So you can find
 the one line
  already written
   inside you.

Sometime with
 the bones of the black
  sticks left when the fire
   has gone out

someone has written
 something new
  in the ashes
   of your life.

David Whyte <u>The House of Belonging</u>
—from "The Journey"

THE COUPLE

I saw a pair
of red-wing blackbirds.
He strutted
showed his importance.
He bossed
you go there
you stand here
you eat only of this.
She tired of his antics.
She flew away.
He followed.

THUNDER AND FLUTE

I crave the thunder
the roll, the black.
I want to feel
it under my ribs.
Feel the boom,
the one that comes
with the rain.

Have you ever heard
a flute
in the rain?
The sound pure,
so sweet.
Then the crack,
then the rain.
The sweet longing
of that flute
calling the thunder back.

Le Tonnerre et la Flûte

Je désire ardemment le tonnerre
le roulement, le noire
Je veux le sentir
sous mes côtes.
Sentir le grondement,
celui qui vient
avec la pluie.

Avez-vous jamais entendu
une flute
dans la pluie?
Le son pur,
si doux.
Puis le claquement,
après la pluie.
Le désir doux
de cette flûte
rappelant le tonnerre.

Between the Heart and the Belly

Between the heart and the belly
under my ribs
is where the quickening comes.
That soft roll of life.
Almost can't feel it, but
I know it's there.

I had it when my babies
lay inside me. That first
moment I knew them.
It's the quickening.

I felt it when a piece of art worked
when I didn't know how.
A piece so beautiful in my mind
I could not let go and I quivered inside.

One day I lost it through my despair.
Sickness, then death
and loneliness came in
and my quickening stopped.
I gave up, just quit trying.
And I died inside.

Found it, felt it by the fire.
Couldn't identify, forgot its name.
Did not remember what it was
only that it was gone.
I did not know her.

I knew something was there.
For weeks she kept caressing me
from the inside. Wouldn't stop.
I tried to understand, find her again.
I knew, I knew her.

I hunted for the name.
Quickening, quickening
my body exclaimed.

I remembered, and listened.
I sat by that fire
held my soul in my hands, felt it shudder.
And my body breathed,
said, "Thank you, you found me again".

I went through heat and ice,
dark and light
but my quickening stayed with me.
I found my sexuality, got it back
from the petal and stamen
of a Calla Lily.

Held my soul in my hands.
Saw my spirit break free
into thousands of feathers
that blow in the wind, float in the breeze.

I began my journey
drove a thousand miles to be alone.
Found words, blessed words.
They opened me up, gave me life again.

Stayed in a cabin, me and my thoughts.
Walked the beach of my beloved ocean.
Smelled that smell of forest decay
and wrote.

My soul gave me muse, my spirit dropped
feathers.
I picked a feather from the wind.
Turned it to a pen.
Filled it with the blood
of my heart
and I wrote and wrote again.

My soul stayed open, I wrote of grief
then hope and letting go.
It spoke, encountered me on my own ground.
Said it was time for me to move on.
And I wrote of that too.

My words were fire, fear and bile.
They frightened me.
I wrote them anyway
and my anger, my fears dissipated.
Words broke the chains that bound me to
grief.

When I cannot speak or find the words
I take up a pen and write –
    How do I say
        or how do I tell
and ink flows from my pen.

Came back to the tree where I had
left my lover.
Wrote of my journey
and now of my letting go, able to move on.
My insides flutter. I know I am alive again.

THE CANYON

The canyon is narrow, so long.
But it is safe.
I see forward, and back.
I look upward, the walls are high.
No danger there.
I look down, at the ground,
it is smooth. I can walk,
I will not stumble.
I just have to take one step at a time.

The earth quakes, I shudder.
My canyon has crazed.
Deep fissures have opened.
I know not where to go.
I must move on.
I cannot stay there.
How? A step at a time.

I step. I plod.
I cry, "Oh my God, Why?"
I walk. The canyon walls
begin to part.

One side catches the sun,
is warm, teems with excitement.
The other lives in darkness
with the moon.
It is not of death, but of fear.

My path flows
from left to right and back.
Each time I cross, the canyon widens.
I am not so afraid of either side now.
This is my life.
I must walk it.
One step at a time.

I Wander

I wander
what do I see.
A bee, feeding
on the lace of flowers.
An old tree
sharing food and shelter.

I see swallows
soaring through the morning
and evening skies.
Two stay behind
begin their beginning.

The sea kisses the shore
never tires of her.
The osprey, the wind
meet and dance.

The clouds
stroke the mountains.
I see the sun
and it watches me
as I wander.

THE PUPPIES SAY

I have settled
out of my tears.
The puppies want
me to scratch their ears.

They say life
goes on. Get busy.
I need food
and I want to run.
Find another
time to brood.

I Talk

I am excited, terrified.
I want to talk, to share,
to give of me.

I lie here,
I tremble, I fear.
I want to be heard.
But what will they hear?

Will they understand?
Will they see
they are of me?

When the stories are told
what will they think?
Will the monsters
under the bed
be put to sleep?

When they see the light
through my broken shell.
Will they hear that I love them
and always will.

How Far

How far does one
need to run to be free?

Is a thousand miles
far enough?

Do I still need
a little more distance?

THE TIDES OF MY LIFE

I learned to open.
Richard, Soulcraft[1], they taught me.
It hurts, but it lives
this openness.

I grow, my words become true.
Pieces form in my mind
pushed out with my tongue.

My soul is heavy,
tired sometimes.

I remember to be open
to listen, to see.
I no longer sob.
The tears fall,
glide from my eyes.

These tides of my life.
The feelings ebb and fall.
My memories cry.
My salt mixes.

The pools collect
taken by the next tide.
And I begin again.

1. Bill Plotkin Soulcraft

THE PIECES OF MY SOUL

This journey pulls at my mind,
my soul, my hands.
I want to wander, have no rules.

To not be afraid, to be afraid.
To work through that fear.
I know, what is on the other side
is worthwhile.

I want to capture the tears.
They are of –
   loneliness
      sadness
         hunger.
They are of –
   love
      hope
         my quickening.

All the pieces of my soul.
My time.

My Soul Speaks

I lie open, exposed.
My soul speaks to me.
Feel me, be me,
let me be you.
I will love you, if you let me.

Do not be afraid.
I will love you, if you let me.
Let me caress you.
Let me hold you.
I will love you, if you let me.

I will take you to ecstasy,
if you let me.
I will take you to heights
you have never known,
if you will love me.

I will bring you calm, serenity.
I will love you, if you let me.

Always Forward

One moment
I feel,
I am able to float
on the surface of a lake.
Then I am mired
in mud up to my knees,
barely able to move,
having to go forward.

The journey
always is forward.
I get caught in the light
and the dark of the past.

So quickly the forward
is the past.
I must move past it
to go forward again.

MY SOUL BROUGHT ME GIFTS

My soul brought me gifts tonight.
A spiral
of pearls and blue stones.
A mound
knitted together of pearls,
flecked with stones
of purple and green.
He gently laid them
upon my womb.

He built a warp of copper,
forever in my loin.
He wove
brown and cream pearls,
and studded them
with stones
of green and amber.
These he bound to me
for eternity.

He brought me breath
to speak.
And Anasazi art,
to remember to touch again
those who touch me.

He tells me
the wind and the oceans

are gifts,
but the earth is of me
and I of it.

I Draw My Breath

As I draw my breath
I smell that smell.
The one of sand and salt
of water,
of woods and ponds and creeks.
All here, bound in God's creations.

The wind messes with my hair
and gives me all of this in a breath.

I go to the edge of this beloved sea.
The wind whips me, blasts me.
Tells me to remember where I am
and who I am with.

I step in the foam.
It is cold, but delicious.
It swirls about my toes.

I hunt for shells
for flat stones, for agates.
I step in deeper.
It is around my ankles,
begins to pull me.
A little deeper
I know it is not safe.

She would pull me in
never let me leave
or spit me out on distant sand.

My Soul Says Open

My soul says, Open for me.
I say, I am not ready.
He says, Yes
and the time is now.

I say, No, I am not ready.
He says, Yes, you promised.
I whimper. He says, Now

I want to show you now.
I open, my world rocks.
Why ever did I wait so long?

IT JUST IS

The waves, the sand
the grasses and the trees
even the frog
the elk and the osprey
try to teach me.
They say, "It just is."

The sea must kiss
and stroke the shore.
The wind must run
her fingers
through the tall sea grasses.
She must howl through the firs.

The rain will caress the frog
and he will croak lovingly.
The sun shines
on the feathers of the osprey.
The wind carries her
to dizzying heights
and turns her loose to soar.

The croak of the frog is as important
as the bugle of the elk.
The blackberry's flower
is as beautiful as the wild Rody.

I must listen to nature's creatures.
To hear the wind.

To love the rain
and the sun equally.
Each has its time, its place.
So do I.

My Soul Hangs Out There

My loins ache.
A constant feeling
of loneliness, of wanting.
I think my soul hangs out there.
I hear
   crying
      wishing
         hope.
He wants me
I want him.
We are close
Our dance begins.

I Am Alone

The crow is cawing to be busy.
My mind, my body want to rest.
I am learning to live
within myself
and I think that is
an important lesson.

I listen to music
the love songs.
I wonder if I will ever feel
that type of love again.
It almost destroyed me.

Still, I wish for that ache.
For the laughter of new love.
I do not want the pain.
I just want to laugh that way.

How do you share
the closing of the day
and the opening of the dawn?
The human heart is not
meant to live alone.

What do the species
that mate for life do
when they lose their other?
What does the goose do

when her other
is shot from the sky?

The elephants, when old age
takes one to its knees
what is the other to do?

Can a goose cry?
Is the trumpet we hear
that of grief?
Do they look to nature
to fill them, again?
What can fill them, heal them?
I want to know
I need to know.

I have felt so brave
so courageous.
I laughed and danced
in the rain.

Now tonight I cry.
I want these tears
to mean something.

I'm afraid of being
alone, forever.
Can I fill what I need
by myself?

This journey is teaching me
to be open to nature.

To feel and see her.
To delight in her antics.

From the croak of the frog
to the roar of the ocean
I can hear the grandeur.

I do not shrink from the wind.
I am embracing the rain
and I love the mist.

I talk to the elk, the trees.
I watch the birds and laugh.

But still I am alone.
I do not belong to these things.
I know I am part, and I am trying.
But my longing is elsewhere.

It is dark now.
All I want is to cry.

I Am Here God

There is a hair shirt
under my blouse of silk.

Oh, to be able
to remove them both.
To feel the breath of the wind
and the wet of the rain
upon my breast.

To be able to beat my chest
to say, "I am here God.
You made me.
In all your glory
You made me. Me
my own ignoblest of self."

I want to feel life
not scratched and torn
by what I did
and did not do.

I want to live forward
always forward
to promise and hope.

I want to be drawn as moths
to that final flame
of my own immortality.

To the light that follows death.
And find where the frog's croak
meets eternity.

MEMORY ROAD
in memory of Bill Gaskill

I drive this road alone
no, not really alone.
Me, and the memories
of my beloved and I.

The aspen so sweet.
Spring, tiny buds
summer, glorious green
fall, oh, you have to see
the sun shining through
translucent leaves.
Winter, the white bark
branded with black bands.
He loved them
no matter the season.

The meadow where we lie
in a field of −
wild daisies
    white yarrow
        yellow buttercups.
I hear our laughter
feel our smiles
lazy
important only
in our togetherness.

I remember the drive

CAMINO DE RECUERDOS
en memoria de Bill Gaskill

Conduzco este camino sola
no, no verdaderamente sola.
Yo, y mis recuerdos
de mi querido y yo.

Los álamos tan dulces.
La primavera, los brotes pequeñísimos
el verano, verde glorioso
el otoño, ay, tienes que ver
el sol brillando por
hojas translucientes.
El invierno, la corteza blanca
marcada con franjas negras.
Él los amó
no importa la estación.

El prado donde nos tumbamos
en un campo de –
Margaritas silvestres
   la milenrama blanca
      los ranúnculos amarillos.
Oigo nuestra risa
siento nuestras sonrisas
perezozos
importantes solo
en nuestra unión.

Recuerdo la vuelta

through the cottonwoods
that last fall.
Him so frail.
The golden essence
made us stop
and just look
for a sweet moment.

Now in spring
their cotton blows across me
touches me
reminds me
the seasons go on.

por los algodones
ese último otoño.
Él tan frágil.
La esencia dorada
nos hizo parar
y solo mirar
por un momento dulce.

Ahora en la primavera
su algodón sopla sobre mí
me toca
me recuerda
las estaciones continuan.

My Psyche and My Soul

He says the psyche
will give me
no more than I can bear.
I feel my soul
and believe that too.
It will not allow me
to be destroyed.

The psyche, the mind
The soul, the heart
They protect me
but they do not isolate me.

They tell me –
　　to think
　　　　to feel
　　　　　　to not quit
　　　　　　　　to trust
　　　　　　　　　　to fight
　　　　　　　　　　　　to believe.

I hear them.
I will survive.
Each blow I take
will strengthen me
and someday, maybe

my psyche, my soul
will say, well done.

— CHAPTER FOUR —

I want to step through the door full of curiosity, wondering:
what is it going to be like, that cottage of darkness?

When it is over, I want to say: all my life
I was a bride married to amazement.
I was the bridegroom, taking the world into my arms.

Mary Oliver <u>New and Selected Poems</u>
—from "When Death Comes"

THE STORM

I lie here, listen
to the sound of the storm.
Hear the crack of thunder
that fills me.

I stood in the wind
and felt the power,
the glory of her.

She pounds the night.
Ribbons of light,
flashes fill the sky.

And then
that beloved crack.
The tearing of the sky
ripping it apart.
The sound rolls through me.
The bass, that can go no lower.

It fills my soul.
Somehow mending me.

HE GIVES ME VOICE
for Richard Hiester

I have a friend.
Where I can speak.
Say anything.
Not shock him.
Well, maybe a little.
Not be judged.

Where my soul can lie
open, exposed.
Where my mind
has free rein, to soar
over mountains,
write a poem.

A friend who quietly
cheers me on.
Who hopes for me.
Who believes my dreams.

He pushes my limits.
Tells me, I can do more.
He helps me
open my heart again
so I can feel, find
my passions. Yes, plural.

To pick up a pen.
To write of childhood –

Il me Donne la Voix
à Richard Heister

J'ai un ami.
Avec qui je peux parler.
Dire n'importe quoi.
Ne pas le choquer.
Eh, bien, peut-être un peu.
Je ne suis pas jugée.

Où mon âme peut rester
ouvert, exposée.
Où mon esprit
a la liberté de s'élever
au-dessus les montagnes,
écrire un poème.

Un ami qui silencieusement
 m'acclame.
Qui espére pour moi.
Qui croit mes rêves.

Il pousse mes limites.
Me dit, je peux en fair plus.
Il m'aide
ouvrir mon cœur une fois de plus
tellement que je peux sentir, rencontrer
mes passions. Oui, pluriel.

Prendre une plume.
Écrire de l'enfance—

of pain
of passion
of soul.
To push clay
through my fingers.
Wet and firm, it can be
anything I choose it to be.

Color –
Chartreuse
lemon yellow
reds
and blue.

Will they be –
of cloth
of paper
of paint?

Or is it my garden
that I see?
This sight, he has
given it back to me.

He knows me, as no other.
He has walked with me –
on dangerous trails
on rocky roads
on busy streets.
We traverse creeks
stand at the shore.

de la douleur
de la passion
de l'âme.
Pousser la pâte à modeler
entre mes doigts.
Mouillée et fermée, cela peut être
ce que je choisis d' être.

Couleur —
Chartreuse
jaune citron
rouges
et bleu.

Seront-ils—
de tissu
de papier
de peinture?

Ou, est-ce que c'est mon jardin
que je vois?
Cette vue, il m'en
a rendu à moi.

Il me connaît, uniquement
Il a marché avec moi—
sur pistes dangereuses
sur routes rocheuses
sur rues occupées.
Nous traversons les ruisseaux
nous restons à la côte.

He does not lead me by the hand.
He stands beside me
and follows.
He waits.
He gives me voice.
I speak.

Il ne me mene pas par la main.
Il reste à côté de moi
Il me suit.
Il m'attend.
Il me donne la voix.
Je parle.

I WAR WITHIN MYSELF

I war within myself.
I want to love
feel that sweet passion.
To care for another.

My next breath says, never again.
Too much hurt, too many nettles.

Could I push
my remembrances aside?

Would I break out in tears
if my cheek was brushed,
just so?

Would I flinch, scalded
from a touch
on my breast?

Could I allow
him to undress me?
Not feel the touch
come through the decades
of so long ago?

I do not have an answer.
So my mind, my body
say just fuck.

Find someone who does not care.
Who will not be gentle
or look into my eyes.

I do not want my soul exposed.
I do not want to meet his mind.

Except,
that I do.

A Drop of Dew

There is hope
in this drop of dew
that falls from my eyes.

The shape magnifies
the hope, the word
sparkles inside.

I will live again
hold a lover to my breast
feel again in my heart.

I don't know how.
I've never hunted before.
Can I be a huntress?

I don't know
I never tried.
It just came easy.
Maybe too easy.

ASHER'S PICTURES

Almost every time I wake
I shake.

Is that a dove or raven
in my chest that beats me?

I dream. I keep
hearing truth
truth, only truth.

I am afraid.
What rides those wings?

I hear
Asher's mother—
"You should make
the world pretty Asher."[2]
And Asher's—
"It's not
 a pretty world Mama."

2. Chaim Potok, <u>My Name Is Asher Lev</u>

I Am Content
for my daughters Laura and Lisa

It was hot today
but this evening the air is
smooth and warm.

We saw winged creatures.
Lisa wanted them
to be bats
I wanted birds.

Lisa said, "The bats
are wonderful."
Laura said,
"They have rabies."
My dreamer
my pragmatist.

They speak as equals
the two years between
now gone.

My heart aches
in the most
delicious way
to hear, to feel
their essence.

The laughter
is wonderful here.

The easiness
we have fallen into.

The talk of spiders,
Black Widows.
The beauty of the
black bubble.

One child says,
"Step on it."
The other says, "No,
only if it is where
it can harm."

Loving, listening
rebuilding, regifting
of the moments.

Singing songs we sang
as children to our children
and they to theirs.

Both women remembering
the reading of the books.

Me remembering
the sitting
on the couch with
a child on each side.
Knowing that the stories
kept them beside me.

I did something right.
I am so blessed.
I am content.

My only confusion is wanting
the time to write.
To not lose this feeling.

Knowing I must
put the pen down.
Take the time to live,
that which I wish
to write about.

These words have
become music to me.
I hear myself –
my voice now.

Today my children
fill me. My cup is full.

I want to
hear them speak
laugh, tell their tales.

Hear their remembering.
Feel them in my soul.

Each one unique.
Only of themselves
but still, they are of me.

Tonight, I look over at
two tousled heads
on white pillows.

They look so innocent
like before
when they were young.
I'm amazed
I feel the same
as when they were small.

I lie in the dark
they talk and I smile.
I can not tell by the voices
which one is speaking
only by the content of their thoughts.

The soft purr of sleep
is music to my ears.
Tonight
I am full again.

ASHER, TEACH ME

Asher
I cry, teach me.

It is not the disapproval
I fear.

It is the pain in his eyes
that I cannot bear.

From the sheltered life
to what?

I hear the collective cheers
and then that single tear.

Oh, Asher
teach me.

Chaim Potok <u>My Name Is Asher Lev</u>

The Poetry Reading

I bare my soul.
I will be brave.

How much soul can
I let others see?
Why do I wish
to speak?
Why do I want
to hide?

I like –
    my words
        my emotions
            wants
raw upon the page.

Maybe, speaking
out loud
is cathartic. Maybe

the gashes
in my soul will
scab, begin to heal. Or

if I pick at the wound,
will it fester?

I listen with
my ears, hear
with my heart.

The letters
　　dripping
　　　drifting
　　　　pouring
into words.

The words
to poems sending
shafts to my heart.

I saw laughter.
It may be blueberry
colored forever
in my mind.

The words matter.

Women abused
　　cut
　　　bruised
　　　　broken.
Once hidden
today exposed.
The power of now.

The Chicana movement.
Powerful, sad.
The love
of culture, heritage.
They were vulnerable, raw.

The worry of nuclear
holocaust, to
the cigarette
butt on the ground.

The young boy
frightened to silence
at the border.
Cannot remember
his name, his age.
His father taken
from him. Nothing
else mattered. Only
to get him back.

I saw how a few
words placed just right
can stay forever.
Driven into
a stranger's heart.

I will always
remember a woman
standing nude
upon her head,
inviting her lover in.

She gone.
Only remembrance,
her essence, her scent
remains.

The laughter
   the longing
     the sharing
just so someone
knows he, she, lived.
Oh yes, they lived.

Read my erotica.
So frightened
I shook.
But another part glad
gave me wings.
Reminded me of
love past
potential of again.

I blushed,
turned scarlet
when I heard
the erotic haiku.
Seventeen syllables
of pure sex. Words
parried. I have
never heard those
words in that order.
Funny, hot.

The closing.
The poetry
of prayer. Yes
I was affected.

I want to give wild
sunflowers to birds
longing, yearning for
withered sun.

I want to give
children love
of words strung together.
   To read
      write
         feel
this world of letters turned
to words.

I am sated, satisfied.

I Think Quiet Thoughts

My body is older
does not spring so well.
I am more careful
the easy balance gone.

My mind, not so sharp.
I forget what I'm saying.
What was I getting
ready to do?
What was I going to get?

Oh for the blessing of youth.
Always –
   moving
      thinking
         planning.
The hustle
the quick beat of life.

I think quiet thoughts.
Not better ones
but more deliberate.
More of me
and what surrounds me.
Now I write
and live my thoughts.

I am slower.
I walk carefully.

I know, I am frail.
Broken bones
do not mend so well,
not so easily.

I do not need so much.
But will not settle for less.
I know my time is measured.
So I will smile more.
Find my hugs, my kisses.
Think my quiet thoughts.

Have You Ever

On a winter's night
with snow on the ground.

Have you ever cooked –
    bits of steak
        Kielbasa
            or little Smokies
on a stick
    in a fire
        in your house?

Smelled the smoke
    of Piñon
        Apple
            or Oak.

Have you sunk into
the soft sweet smell
of leather?
Kicked off your shoes,
pulled your toes
in under yourself?

Drunk a glass or two
of dark red wine
or White Zinfandel?

Have you read,
written, poetry
by candlelight?

Yours, mine, both.
The words –
     honey sweet
          lemon tart
               icy cold.

Would you roast
marshmallows
to a golden brown?
Eat a Macintosh
with sharp
cheddar cheese,
or both?

A New Skin

I am so ready to love again.
I sat through my grief
my loneliness.
In my memories I hold
the love of my life.

But now I must
step forward, step out.
I need to stroke my life.
The one that is in front of me.

I need to caress
be caressed,
my body craves this
but so does my mind.
My soul wants to
unfurl its wings,
spread them wide.

It wants to soar, drift
on the currents of wind
as the Osprey do.

My mind needs to reach
touch the poet.

My hands want the touch of clay.
It is so elementary, this mud.
It is slick, wet, smooth, void of shape.

But in my fingers it takes shape
becomes a vessel, a form.
It is faces and bears,
bowls for serving,
cups for my tea.

Fabric glows and caresses my skin.
It is of cotton, silk, wool.
Each has a place.
I cut, sew, cut again.
Restitch again, over and over
till it is right.

The fibers, the thread
bind me.
Tie me to my truth.
It must be of me.
It cannot be a lie.

I sit in the middle of my life.
The shards and pieces
are at my feet.
Pieces of prose circle my head.

How do I take these pieces,
these threads and create?
How do I create
a cloak, a new skin?

I Will Live

I will write
while the words come.
See color
while my eyes still shine.

Push clay into shapes
that please me.

I will touch, feel texture
of rock, and wood.

Nature will entice me.
She will scream –
   Look at me!
     No!
       Really!
         See me!

Sleep in my bed of moss.
   Feel—
      open your skin
        delicious rain
           sweet soft wind
              warming sun
I give you.

I will hold those most dear to me.
I will live as if tomorrow will
never be.

Just Beginning to Feel

I shake hands.
What do I say?
Can I, do I want
to small talk.
I'm just beginning to feel again.

I have to shop.
T-shirts and jeans are my style.
I don't want the frills.
I want to be female.
I don't know about feminine.

Right now, I need a poet
so I can speak, use my voice.

Maybe.

THE HERE, THE NOW
for Kathy Rochau

The here, the now
is all there is.
No matter the past,
not even the promise
of tomorrow.

If we spend the now
living in the past,
we miss this moment.

If we only wish
to be elsewhere,
we forget to look
at the here –
be it exciting or bare.

If this is all there is
will we live it
with honor, clarity?

If there is more,
will we take a step,
cross a line,
leap a chasm,
soar to eternity?

Is eternity tomorrow, forever?
Or is it always here, always now.

Dan Millman <u>Way Of The Peaceful Warrior</u>

Marching of Time

I do not feel sadness
for the marching of time.
But I am aware
as never before
how much time remains.

Will I at least
leave a scuff mark?
Or will I be
that hand in a bucket of water,
pulled out
and nothing changed.

I do not need
to change the world.
But a little ripple
would be nice.
To be known
and remembered
Just a little.

WINTER'S FIRE

It is time for the first
fire of the season.
Tomorrow I will wake.
The wood waits.
I will light a match
touch it to paper—
my winter flame will begin.

As I sit inside and
listen to howling winds,
where will my mind go?

Will I visit Jung and Philemon?
Will Plotkin take me
to soul again?
Will another chapter of my journey
take shape?

Will the smell of smoke
glow of embers
bring me to poetry?

I love winter days
trapped inside.
On these days
I like myself
hear my soul
feel my beat.

So tonight I sleep.
Tomorrow
I will strike that light
and I will speak.

C. G. Jung <u>The Red Book</u>
Bill Plotkin <u>Soulcraft</u>

It Is Now

The now
is an hour before daybreak.
It could be morning,
brightness of day,
dusk, dark of night.

What do I do with each moment?
Do I cry, laugh
write, journal
create music of words.
Do I garden, sleep?

How many types of sleep are there?
The sleep of tears, of happiness,
of exhaustion, just rest.

My writing, the words so raw,
sometimes they make me fall asleep.
When I wake I see them clear.

Rewrite them again and again
so many agains.
But then it is right
and I dream them again
when I sleep.

So often I am driven
and I bring the
past to light and

I live and feel the pain and joy
and it becomes the now.

I feel the touch of my lover.
His arms reaching,
holding me while I cried and
I cry in the now.
Taste the salt
mixed with the sweet cool
and warmth of his mouth.

Feel his arms
as he pulls me to his chest.
Feel the sobs rack my body
as his breath
moves through my hair
till I am still.

I write of oceans and canyons
that I have seen,
and I use them now.

All this is my song today.
I love these remembrances
even those that hurt
but no longer harm me.

I have afternoons of meadows.
Sometimes walking
often lying,
grasses tickling,
caressing my body.

I have memory of morning love
the lazy wake up.
Arms reaching
tracing my love's face
with sleepy fingertips.

Now I write
and I hope in days to come
someone, somewhere
will read my words
and feel what I did.

Understand the heat of sun,
caress of wind.
See the fingers of light,
feel the clutch of thunder.
Understand and know me.

CHRIST, SHEEP, CHILDREN

I sit in my pew
look up at that blank cross.
Wonder at the pain inflicted.

I see the stained-glass
of my youth –
   Christ
      sheep
         and children.
I was content in my innocence.

The sins done
in my Savior's name.
And before
when Cain struck Able.

Hitler
   Stalin
      the Crusades
         now ISIS
            Hezbollah
               Hamas.
The Christian quakes inside.

But still I feel as that child
crawling up to sit
upon his lap.
Feel his essence
hear his words.

SPEAK POET SPEAK

The truth wins out.
I think of Asher,
truth always truth.

Of Richard,
if it's not of truth
it's not worth writing.

Each day I struggle.
I listen.
I write of dreams
past and future.

The truth of the past,
the bruises,
also the kisses.

The touch of baby's skin.
The smell of the powder.
The cry, the fear
when I cannot hold her.

The love of a man
turned bitter and cruel.

Then the lover
who caresses,
opens my heart,
my soul, my mind.

My world becomes larger
I grow each day.
I will ride the wind
dance in the sun.
I will be the poet.
I will speak.

Chaim Potok <u>My Name is Asher Lev</u>

A Ghost in the Mist

I say –
    I love you,
        I want to love you,
            Love me,
to a ghost in the mist.

I do not know
who he is.
An entity that
makes my heart
ache with longing.

I say, Please
make love to me.
I feel his
fingers slide
down my arm
encircle my waist.

I lean to him.
I feel his breath
in my hair.
Hear it catch
as he breathes in
the honeysuckle
of me.

I can't see him.
    Just feel him.

I want him
to stay.

He's drifting away.
Oh, please
come stay with me.

What Is My Life to Become

What is my life to become?
Are these emotions
ever be acted upon?

I am so capable of love.
How do I share it?
I want to be excited when I awake.
I want to feel arms around me
and breathe in essence of male.
I want to be excited, content
and excited again.

Right now, this moment,
I am content, quiet
but something inside
flutters to be free.

I want to lay my head
on his chest.
Who is he?
I want to hear his voice
muffled in my hair.

Decide what will happen
during each day
for each of us, separately.

Breaking away
knowing that dusk

will bring us back together.
Darkness, back to entwinement
excitement, contentment.

He Was a Fantastic Lover

I feel the silken rope
around my wrist.
I am his.

I want to acknowledge our love,
our lovemaking.
It was beauty, sensuality.
Whipped cream and strawberries
were funny, hot.

Erotica not here on these pages
but it existed.
Denial is not what I wish for,
not here, in my truth.

That telling is for another space.
Here I will use the illusions,
the mountain meadows.

But I want to shout
from the rooftops that
he was a fantastic lover.
He was kind, gentle,
thoughtful and thoroughly loving.

Maybe that says enough.
This is part of my loss, my grief
and I want to tell it.

It's Time for Me to Go On

I picked up his picture.
I traced my finger
on the curve of his face.
Gently told him, it's time
for me to go on.

Not fast
not careening
but if I am asked
"Would I like a coffee"
I should go.

That my sensual side
is somehow still alive.
I hear music again.
I see light.
I allow wind to touch me
as I write. I think
I'm ripe again.

Thank You, Babe

I spent tonight
smiling and laughing.
Not like before, but
this was acceptable.

I thought of him
talked of him
but it was all right.

I told sexy stories
to strangers, but it
was my story
my laughter, my caresses
my time.

Thank you, Babe
for the memories.

SECOND SECTION

There is so much more to who you are than you know right now. You are, indeed, something mysterious and someone magnificent. You hold within you – secreted for safekeeping in your heart – a great gift for this world.

—Bill Plotkin <u>Soulcraft</u>

THE SUN AND THE SEA

I saw them flirting
all afternoon.
She smiled at him.
He threw off
his mantle of gray.

She cast diamonds
upon his skin.
He laughed
and rolled to the shore.
She laughed back, said,
"You can do better."

She brightened his smile
with her kiss of warmth.
He frolicked and roared
and threw gifts
on the shore.

She moved closer.
He enticed her.
She changed his color
to golden.
He grew dark
mysterious.
She had to see.
He ate her.

FLOSSIE (ENGLISH)
in memory of Flossie Jaramillo

I miss Flossie
all four feet eleven and one half inch
of her.
She the matriarch of the family.
She held her arms out
said, "welcome m'hija".
I had never been held
that way, that hard.

I was a little afraid but
I had to go back.
Who could not desire that
which she offered so freely?

We broke tortillas together.
She taught me to make
red chile, green chile stew,
beans with chicos,
carne adovada, natillas.

I learned to pick wild asparagus
by the river,
find and cook lamb's quarters
and pig weed.

From that culture, I learned
to butcher, do the matanza.
I learned to use everything

FLOSSIE (ESPAÑOL)
en memoria de Flossie Jaramillo

Echo de menos a Flossie
todos los cuatro pies y once y media pulgadas
del ella.
Ella es la matriarca de la familia.
Ella extendió sus brazos
dijo, —bienvenidos, m'hija—.
Yo nunca he sido abrazado
en esa manera, tan fuerte.

Yo tenía un poco de miedo pero
Yo tenía que regresar.
¿Quién no podía desear lo
que ella ofreció tan libremente?

Rompimos tortillas juntas.
Me enseñó a cocinar
chile rojo, caldito de chiles verdes,
frijoles con chicos
carne adovada, natillas.

Aprendí a coger espárragos trigueros
al lado del río,
encontrar espinacas quelites
y verdolagas.

De esa cultura, aprendí a hacer
la carnicería, hacer la matanza.
Aprendí a utilizar todo

from a hog, losing only
the hair and the squeal.

Making the chicharrones
always stirring to the right.
The joy of eating them hot
wrapped in tortillas.

I remember
I still smell the smoke,
feel the cool of autumn morning.
My children played in the barn.
Rolled in the hay.

Called Tio, Uncle Tio
he just smiled.
Never corrected them.
It just became his name.

I bucked bales of hay.
Rode my horse on the bush tracks.
Danced the western dances
till I would drop.

Partied and worked at their celebrations.
The weddings, the baptisms,
first Communions, coming of age.
I loved the beauty, the colors,
the crinoline, the laughter and the sounds.

Flossie loved me 'til the day she died.
I loved her back with equal fervor.

de un cerdo, sólo perdiendo
el pelo y el chillido.

Preparando los chicharrones
siempre removiendo a la derecha.
La alegría de comerlos calientes
envueltos en tortillas.

Yo recuerdo
todavía el oler del humo,
siento el frescor de la mañana otoñal.
Mis hijas jugaron en la granera.
Se revolcaron en el paja.

Llamaron a Tío, tío Tío
sólo sonrió.
Nunca las corrigió.
Sólo llegó a ser su nombre.

Alcé balas de paja.
Monté mi caballo por las pistas de carreras.
Bailé los bailes del oeste
hasta no poder más.

Fuí de fiestas y trabajé a sus celebraciones.
Las bodas, los bautismos,
primeras comuniones, quinceañeras
Me encantaron la belleza, los colores,
la crinolina, las risas y los sonidos.

Flossie me amó hasta el día en que se murió.
Le devolví el amor a ella con fervor igual.

I miss those arms that taught me
to love another.

It never mattered
that my hair was coppery red
and hers coal black
with wisps of gray.

Echo de menos esos brazos que me enseñaron
a amar a un otro.

Nunca le importó a ella
que mi pelo era cobrizo
y el suyo era negro como carbón
con mechones de gris.

Star Over Abiquiu

One of the most
beautiful sights
I have ever seen
is the pinnacles of stone,
moon bathed
silhouette.
And a single star
over Abiquiu.

He Had No Right

It wasn't his.
He had no right
to steal
from one so small.

He was so big.
She had to hide.
He was so tall
the biggest
of them all.

How could she fight?
She could not run.
She could not tell.
She was so little.
Shush
she must be still.

And she grew.
She did not tell.
Twenty years come and gone.
Two children, two husbands
And still it's wrong.

A man looked her up and down.
She was smart.
She was pretty.
She must have "made" him
check her out.

A slap, a punch
knocked her down.
A kick to the stomach
the pull of her hair
the gun at her head
taught her to be still.
The fear, the anger
and the dread.

He was so big.
She had to hide.
He was so tall
the biggest
of them all.

How could she fight?
Who would believe?
She could not run.
Nowhere to flee.
She was ashamed.
She could not tell.
So she stayed
locked in her cell.

Now forty years
have come and gone.
She is old, no longer pretty.
But still, she's smart.

She stands before you –
   no longer runs
      she does not fear

        she does not hide.
She has pride—
      her dignity
         her voice.

He was so big.
She had to hide.
He was so tall
The biggest of them all.

I Curse

I knew, it was too good
to be true.
The light, the laughter
(Where is my laughing man now?)
have been wiped away
in a moment.
What is the price?

I am at the dark side
of the canyon. Remember,
it is not death. It is fear.
Where is the joy
the balance?

I cry, I tear.
I want to break something
anything.
I curse (I don't do that)
Yes I can!
I do.
   Damn
      Damn
         Damn!
            Fuck!
               Screw it!

I will not break.
He will not win.
This thing, that brings me joy

has brought back, the sorrow.
Has brought back
life's pain and passion.

It is the service
That will bring me joy
and make my soul whole.
And, God willing, take me
from the dark side
and give me light.

Last Night's Moon

Last night the moon
chased the sunset away.
Pillows of gray and purple
were laced with
the gold of the moon.

HUGS

I love hugs except
for the obligatory ones.

When I say I need a hug.
I'm saying care about me.

When I cry
and you hold me,
I ask to stay a little longer
so I can take
your energy and heal.

When I love,
the hug, the clasp
is the one that lasts
through the night.

When we hug goodbye,
it's sharing that essence
till we meet again.

Art Is Breath

Art is breath.
My lungs take baby steps
tiny breaths of fear.
It feels right, good.
Air in
words out.
Deeper breaths
fear replaced by joy.

Oxygen to my mind
thoughts quicken
my fingers tremble.
I pick up the pen.
The lace that I draw,
words today
tangles tomorrow,
the line that turns
to a leaf, a flower.

I thank my God
for breaths today.
For the thoughts
He gives me.
For the words that
tumble from my mind
to my pen, my lips.

L'ART EST LE SOUFFLE

L'art est le souffle.
Mes poumons prennent de petits pas
les petits souffles de peur.
Il me semble bien, bon.
L'aire entre
les mots sortent.
Les souffles profonds
la peur remplacée par la joie.

L'oxygène à mon esprit
mes penséés animent
mes doigts tremblent.
Je prends la plume.
Les dentelles que je trace
mots aujourd'hui
embrouillements demain,
la ligne qui change
à une feuille, une fleur.

Je rends grâce à mon Dieu
pour les souffles d'aujourd'hui.
Pour les pensées
qu'ils me donnent.
Pour les mots qui
tombent de mon esprit
à ma plume, mes lèvres.

I Saw Three Young Men

I saw three young men.
Each one contemplating
the hurt of his own falls.

As a grandmother
I wanted to hold them
pull them to me
say it will be okay.
But they are not mine
and they are so tall.
I want to say
"Shush it will be alright"
and wipe away the tears
or say "Cry
till you can cry no more.
Let your body rack with grief
and then sleep."

Fathers, mothers and lovers
in our hearts
act a certain way.
They walk with us
hold our hand.
They keep us safe.

They caress our bodies
when we are tired and worn.
Watch us as we dive into life.
Hear our cries, "Look at me."

Life is not fair.
Fathers, who should never leave, do.
Sometimes mother's arms
get tired from holding the world.
Lover's eyes that always showed
the way home, can falter,
lose their flicker
and we are alone.

These things tear at our hearts,
rip through our souls
and we cry.

When the tears are done
and the body has sighed.
Look at the world
with your fresh-washed eyes.
Grab with those tired
emotion spent limbs,
and hold tight to your world.
Embrace it with tenderness.
Know your own worth.

You can still have it all.
Just turn it around.
Be the father, the mother,
the son, daughter, lover,
sister or brother.

Remember your pain.
Swear to do better.
Hold your own child

or the child of another.
Walk to the zoo,
count petals of a flower.

Remember, a ball,
no matter the size,
can open a path
from father to son,
brother to brother.

When you see that man,
that woman alone.
Smile.
If they wish,
talk till the moon rises
and gives way
to the morning sun.

I would not presume
to tell you to go on.

But knowing your loss
can help another.
Helping another
can soften your loss.

I hope someday
a spark will fly
from the fire that
burns in your heart,
create a soft glow
of warmth you can move to.

Another heart that beats boldly
wants you to come in.

Feel the pain
but remember the joy.
Find your way.
Find the joy in the sorrow.

HIDY HOLES

There is this tree
you see.
It's pretty big
and it's my favorite tree.
It's an old apple
and we've been friends
for awhile.
He lets me climb
and hang and sleep.

But he has secrets.
He has hidy holes.
You know,
hollow spots
and lots of them.
Yep, lots of them.

I wonder
where they go.
Like,
if I took a marble
and dropped
it in one,
would it come out another?

Like,
if you had a hole
in your pants pocket,
would it fall out

your trouser leg?
Could a tree do that?

Or would it be
like that little hole
in your jacket?
You know,
the one that things go through,
but you can't
get them back.
Would he take my marble
and keep it like that?

It would be cool
if it clanked,
like when we're shooting.

I can't give up my steely
or the one that looks
like the moon.
So it has to be a cat's eye,
the yellow or the blue.

I love the yellow one,
how it spins.
So it's the blue.
I think so.
Which hidy hole?
Does it fit?
Oh, oh.
Gone.

THE CALLA LILY

A Calla Lily
folds upon itself.
One single perfect petal
circles
the phallus, the stamen.

Intertwines him
with perfect longing
and he dusts her with
a golden shower.

The Dark Rainbow

I was feeling
the storm,
enjoying the darkness.
How dare
that rainbow
lift my heart.

TESTOSTERONE
for my grandson Carl

Men, such funny
strange creatures.
I am confounded by their ways.

We adore them in their infancy.
Let them suckle at our breasts.
We watch them, love them.

Some people talk of
the differences
between boys and girls.
Say it is just cultural.

Wrong.

Put them in a meadow.
Little girl pets flowers,
stops to sniff, and glides
through the grasses.

Little boy finds a stick.
Does he even know
he just found a sword?
Whack, whack,
off with their heads,
as he marches forward.

The sports.
That competitive drive.

How many uses
can there be for a ball?

For me, a car
gets me from A to B.
Yes it's nice if it's pretty.
I know the color.
I can locate it
at the store.

But for men,
extensions of their manhood.
Four on the floor
how many horses
the cylinder count does matter.
It may be sleek, sexy,
or tough, to carry
those bales of hay
those cords of wood.
Impress the girls.

Oh, the girls.
Testosterone rush.
The sweet soft
shy smile of the girl.
The holding of hands.
Realization of his power as
he enfolds hers.
Those first honey sweet kisses.

Those first few hairs
that soft fuzz upon his face.

He was always male
now almost man.

He dreams of girls –
    of sports, of girls
        of college, of girls
            the pros, of girls.

In his first cocoon he must
find his survival way –
    scientists
        engineer
            teacher
                blue-collar
                    artist.

With the girls, young women now.
No longer shy.
Still, I think he trembles inside.

The finding of his mate,
please let it be right.
The children. His new role.
He'll make mistakes,
but he'll do alright.

He will balance his
animus with his anima.
To be able to do things
not testosterone-based.

The second cocoon.
His drive, his needs have changed.
He does not need
to wrestle so hard each day
to find food and shelter.

Now can be a quiet time.
The work can meander.
We hope he stands tall,
legs apart, grounded.
Not destroyed by
the fight for life.

The artist, dormant
can now awake.
Hell, even a president
can learn to paint.

Even now the desire to protect
the female, the child.
Testosterone, it is always there.

Why Do Poets Write

Why do poets write?
The obvious, trite answer—
because we have to.
But why?

I write because
I have no choice.
I need to tell my truth.

The words tremble
in my body,
on my tongue.
My mind, sometimes
frightened, terrified.

Banks of fog.
I pull phosphorus
letters from the sea.
I gather them
begin to build the words.
To tell my tale, my truth.

When I am afraid.
It makes me –
    face
        confront
           fight.
I pick, I choose

till it is right
and then I sleep.

But still it is not done.
I say my poetry
gives me voice.
It does.

It requires that I speak
say it out loud. The words
spring to my lips.
Get caught in my tongue.

Sometimes, tastes of bile,
other times, so sweet, so light.

They can be sticky,
grasping to my body,
not wanting to leave
the safety of my lips.

Each time a word is
spoken, a sinew rips,
and it is strengthened.

I am so tired.
I fall asleep.
I can rest.

I wake, I tremble
I write again,
because I have to.

Bed of Moss

I lay on a bed of moss
needing to be alone.
Why does a child of eight
need to be alone?

Today I still remember
that bed
soft and musky,
smell of decaying earth.

I don't remember why,
but that day
I needed to be
cradled,
held by mother earth.

THE DAY LILIES SLEEP

It is morning.
The sun has not yet
climbed the hill.
I hear a crow,
the chirps of small birds.

It is cool out here
almost cold.
The day lilies sleep
not one is open.

The sun is coming—
it will soon be warm.

I will sit here for a while
watch the lilies open.
The sun is just beginning
to touch them.

I can smell the garden
as it opens to the day.

It is the honeysuckle I smell,
delicious, in its fragrance.

My blackberries
are beginning to ripen.
They are so sweet.

The apples, the pears
bend their branches
with their bounty.

Two doves sit
but they are still.

It is quiet, no longer cold.
The lilies begin to open.

I wonder what the birds think,
what they are saying.
Do they like their own sound,
or do they speak?

The doves come and go
but still they are quiet.
Later, I will hear their coos.

The lilies open
in the sun and shadow,
hearing their own
internal clock.

The concrete cool.
I pick up my feet
lie back on the couch.
The sun has reached me.
It is warming my feet.

I feel the tiny breeze.
I see the change in colors
as the sun kisses this earth.

This morning is of little things.
A cup of coffee
a little strudel
the sun rising
(well, I guess that is big).
The bird sounds
changing with the warmth.
The flowers slowly opening,
greeting the new day.

My eyes want to close
to just hear, to smell the essence
of my garden.

I open my eyes.
The day lilies are opening,
some about half.

I fall asleep.
A moth wakes me.
Tells me
I am supposed to watch.

I wonder where the squirrels have gone.
I have not seen them much.
That is of me.
I have not spent my time here.

Morning and night are glorious.
I will spend more evening time here.
I wonder what time
the day lily closes.

I Feel Old Today

I feel old today
spent, used up.

Still, I will shower
get coffee, begin my day.

I will write, rewrite
print my thoughts.

Feel my aches.
Know they feed me.
I will read, feel empathy.

Let my emptiness
take me where it will.

I would not choose
to go back to that
not feeling.

I Have the Right to Believe

Last night
it was said.
Poetry is
the last permissible place –
sex, politics and religion
can be expressed.

I handle the sex
double entendre intended.

Politics drive me crazy.
I am a full blooded
conservative.
I will not change.

I care about the same things
as those left of me.
I just swing a little differently,
take a different path.

Religion—
I sometimes am offended,
but I think in time
I will offend,
do what was done
to me.

My belief
makes me strong.

The Holy Ghost,
God, came to me.
He held me
in my time of need.
Turned my world
to brilliant white.

I love Him so,
do not try
to take Him
from me.

He gave me gifts
that were not there.
Now, I give them
to others.

Have I harmed you?
Do I threaten you?
Do my hymns
hurt your ears?

Does the baby
in a manger,
harm you
each December?

Two pieces of wood
nailed together.
Why do they offend?

I would invite you,
not demand.
Why do you
diminish me?

Have you read
the poetry of the Psalms?
The beauty
of those words?

Give me space.
I do no harm.
I sit in church.
I hear God's word,
acknowledge my sins
eat God's body,
drink his blood.
Pray.

The Diner

I sit here
watching the scotch broom
bounce in the wind.
The river grasses bow
and the willow rocks
to and fro.

I listen
I am inside.
I cannot hear the wind.
But I listen
And I hear the language
of the old.

I am in a diner,
and at sixty-seven
I am the youngest,
except for the cook
and the waitress.

The old men speak of war.
How hard it was.
The respect of the enemy
as he rode to his death.
How it was fought.
There is pride and honor
for a job well done.

The old women pray,
and talk of the sorrow
that few speak to their Lord.
Recipes,
what is in the salad dressing?
What will happen this week
on each day?

The couple.
Mashed potatoes and gravy
the market,
a hamburger,
the weather.
They are quieter,
they know each other,
their sentences are shorter.

I am a stranger here.
I do not belong with them.
But soon
I will be in my own diner
and I will be old.
And concerned
with things of the past
and these little things.

Blackbird, My First Poetry Slam

Blackbird Buvette
Downtown Central, night
black cavernous hole.
I step in.

Music raucous.
Sounds of patrons –
   talking
      drinking
         laughing.
So, out of my comfort zone.

I want to turn, to run.
I had brought my posse of two.
I knew they would stop me if I tried.
So I sidled up to that bar.

I asked in my very polite voice
about The Poetry Slam.
A woman spoke, told me
they were not there yet
should be soon
to sit, to wait.

We found a spot
near the stage
and the door
and I wondered
what I was doing there.

Was I insane?
Only three time have I read
my poems to anyone
except my therapist
and he has to like them.
Only to a group of women
who are my friends.
Drinking tea and coffee.

My music tastes run between
Peter, Paul, and Mary
and Garth Brookes.
I listen to Josh play.
Realize I like his words
and his voice is nice
is good. Loud, but good.

Eric the MC of this group
(I think of him as a Viking)
was nice to me.
Probably horrified, scandalized
when I asked, "What does Slam mean?"

Signed me up in second place.
I think I thanked him.
I went, sat down, eying that door
just a few feet away.

My friends said, "Uh uh
you are not going to run."
I said, "I'm not", but I don't know.

I stared at that stage.
That step looked so tall.

Drank a rum and Coke.
Thank you Josh.
Reminded myself it would
be foolish to be drunk on stage.

Then it began.
Eric at the mic, jokes
bringing me in
making me part of this.
Thanks again Eric.

Then Sarah,
no paper in hand.
Rapid fire words.
I was so frightened
I didn't even hear.
Oh shit!
I could not do that.
I was not prepared.

Eric came to the table.
Told me he needed
to put someone in front of me.
Oh, Thank God!

The man read his poetry, calmly
I began to breathe again.

Then it was, my time.
I made it up that step.
Stood with papers in my hands
and read the story of my journey
through The Canyon lands.

Then I read Hidy Holes.
I knew I would know if people listened
when I finished my final line.

They laughed out loud –
    Oh Yes!
       I will not die.
          I can be here.
          I relaxed
stepped down that step.

Back to my friends.
Rum and Coke tasted so sweet
with a little buzz.

Listened for six more poets
to tell their truths.

People were kind, made me want
to come back. Told me
they liked my poetry.
So here I am back again.
Now, what exactly
is a Slam?

THE WOMEN

The women live
up and down
the street.
Each has a box
with a door.

They sell themselves.
They buy a chance.
They –
    bargain
        steal
            hope
                pray
for the best.

They want –
    pretty
        soft
            safe.

Sometimes they win.
More often –
    slapped down
        bit
            chewed up
                spat out,
by those
designed to protect.

The women
continue to give.
Each generation,
each culture,

knead their bread.
Find the food
to fill their bellies.

They take to their
beds. Want passion
and softness.
Some win,
get to sleep in
his arms, safe
through the night.

Some not so lucky.
Wam Bam
Thank You Ma'am.
Or worse –
    hit
        bit
            torn apart.
Lie in confusion,
in despair.

They gave it all.
Tried to hold
onto their souls.
But some gambled,
lost that too.

I Apologize

for the harm, the pain
I caused.
For shattering his world.

He needs to know that act
was not to punish
nor planned out.
It was my need
not met that
turned me out
to find another.

We talked
heard each other.
Spoke without anger.
Listened with mature ears.

Saw the folly of our youth.
I felt abused and used.
I knew, he did not know
how I had hurt –
   the loneliness
      the expectations
        the work
but mostly the emptiness
of that time.

He says he felt adrift
did not know how to

care for himself.
He waited seventeen years
to find another.
To trust again.

He now is full.
Married again
his life content.

I told my truth
without rancor.
Drew my line.
Now I am done.

The Woodpecker and the Apple Tree

The tree is old, gnarled.
Its skin shot with tiny holes
like freckles.
From his enemy?
From his friend?

The impertinent
woodpecker working,
taking what it wants,
not caring what it wounds.

Still, one feeds, one cleans
and they live
the decades together.

I See the Sea

Each day
the sea begins her dance.
The wind blows
creating flecks
or ropes of white.

The sun throws glitter
diamond dust.
Sometimes so bright
one can barely see.
Other times, enhancing
its perfect beauty.

On a perfect day the sun
breaks out her paintbrush,
tips each wave
with the whitest of white.

Come See Me
for Sandra Layne Gaskill

I want my friend to come
and bake scones with me.
I like them plain
just a hint of sweet.
But I'll have –
chocolate
    raisins
        nuts
to please her palette.

I'll have coffee
she'll have tea.
We'll top it off
with clotted cream.

Summer, we'll sit
outside and watch
dragon and butter flies.
Winter, we'll
curl up on leather,
draw our feet up
feed the fire
watch the flames
and talk.

THE APPLE TREE

I walk on the hillside
behind the cabin.
Wild iris and tall grasses
grow there.

There is an apple tree
at the edge of a meadow.
He is old and gnarled.
Yet, strangely majestic.
He has worked to survive
through injury and disease.

I wonder if any children
hid their treasures
in his hollows.

What birds have crowned his head?
I saw jays peek at me
through his boughs.
The tiniest bird
danced there in the sunlight –
no bigger than a Rufus,
big hummer, small bird.

A Poem Written

Poetry is –
   love
      sex
         politics
           war
or anything else
imaginable.

It is remembrance
of anger
compassion.
It is a story of
kittens and puppies
and monsters under the bed.

Imagine finding a poem
written by an old man
to a woman, his lover
speaking in the language of yore.
   Paper brittle
      brown with age
         ink faded.

The rhymes in a
child's storybook
teach that child to read.

Forever is the image
of your first glimpse

of the sea,
its power, its awe.

The sight of pale lavender.
The wild Pascal flower
in early spring.

Remember that foal
as he hit the ground.
His first gangly effort
finding strength to stand tall.

A poem gives word
to each picture,
each flash of your eyes.
    A hundred
        thousand
            million
minds get to see
because you stopped,
took time, wrote.

FIFTY YEARS AND GROWING
for Bob and Phyllis Gaskill

Two friends together 50 years
plus the courtship time.

I marvel at their strength.
They did not do
what Rilke called
the narrowing of their minds.

They complement.
They grow together
because they have
been allowed
to grow apart.

Their first cocoon—
educated, two children
stability and love.

The second—
beautifully rich,
children grown
with children of their own,
travels, tennis,
hikes and mountain bikes.

I watch them
at this time of life.

Marvel at their presence,
their essence.
They still love.

THE YOUNG OLD

I sit here
baking in the sun.
The leaves are gone
snow has feathered the ground.

You talk of the young old
this is that, my time.

It is delicious
like an apple
allowed to ripen
on the branch.

Clean, crisp,
full bodied flavor.
Color of red,
deep like my blood.

My teeth, still mine,
sink in.
Juices spray,
drip from my mouth
sweetness touches my tongue
sweet liquid
cools my throat.

I love these moments.
They caress.
I live in this old body
it houses my young soul.

My Friends Have Come to Play

Four silky ears, two wet noses
my friends have come to play.

Tyler, a Great Dane
a harlequin, beautifully gray,
with sad eyes and lanky body.

Piper, a Boxer, is energy,
Tight bodied, strong.

Tyler, picks her own apples
from the tree.
Piper, invites
herself in for a swim.

They come, push
their heads under my arm
so I will not forget to pet them.

Their coats, silky smooth
are soothing to my fingertips.
Their insistent kisses
make me laugh.

Yes, these furry creatures
are my friends.
When they go home
I miss them.

LITTLE POET
for Annique

There is a poet.
I know not her name.
I just call her Little Poet.

Her eyes dance,
her body cannot contain
her excitement, her joy.
I see her light up
a fire oozes
from her pores.

She wants to grab hold
onto this part
but a piece is afraid.

Her soul says "Go, start."
But she cries and says
"I am not ready".

Her soul says
"Do not be afraid.
Your time has come.

Your time is now.
Listen, hear, get up.
Be a virgin no more.
Put the pressure
in the right place
and the hymen will break."

It may hurt.
You may tremble.
The fullness burns
but your soul takes wing.
The blood that
lays on your bed
is the ink
that fills your pen.

Write Little Poet.
You write.
It fills you
from the inside
and moves.
It moves as you write
and the writing
moves you.

Little Poet you get
to take a breath.
That moment
has fractured, given you
a hundred thousand seeds,
drops of blood.
Fills your pen
and you begin
to write again.

Camera at the Zoo
for Mixed Media Mavens

A group of artists went to the zoo.
You know, for inspiration.

We all looked
at the same thing that day
we all saw something different.

Bucky, the giraffe,
inspired one woman
to take snippets of weave
to make art of cloth.

Another saw the beauty of
angular features against
New Mexico field of blue.

One saw the grace of eyelashes
as they framed fluid eyes.

One picked up emotion—
The orangutan with her newborn,
such a good mother.

The ape, who just wanted to go home,
dreamed of the mountains
that should have been his.

We all carried cameras.

We thanked God for digital.
We stepped in the sunlight
saw the same in the shadow
and clicked again.
I took over a thousand pictures that day.

I love macro,
to see the veins of the leaves,
the hair of the rope,
the complexity of a knot,

the shininess of a something
that should not have been, but was
dropped to the ground,

the texture of walls, of sticks
of stones, of ground.

One duck, of many, in a pond,
reflections of golden
cottonwood in that same still pond.

After all this time, it still creates.
I see it and now there are words,
this day, enshrined forever
in a poem.

౭౩

About the Author

Ginny Gaskill grew up with the firs, rivers, and oceans of Oregon. At age twenty she traded them for the high desert and canyons of New Mexico.

She spent twenty years involved with the workings of the Los Alamos National Laboratory. There she met her husband Bill and raised her children. Ginny is a widow, mother and grandmother.

For the past twenty-five years Ginny's worked in different art forms, clay, fiber, jewelry, mixed-media, and now words. These words reflect her living. Pain, love, nature, sacredness and humor show up each day as she writes.

ginnyschaos.blogspot.com

www.ingramcontent.com/pod-product-compliance
Lightning Source LLC
Chambersburg PA
CBHW030921090426
42737CB00007B/276